"But It Doesn't Affect Me!"

An Honest Look at the Influence of Entertainment

Al Menconi

www.AlMenconi.com

New Song Publishing

A division of **Al Menconi Ministries**

Carlsbad, CA 92013

"But It Doesn't Affect Me!"

Al Menconi

New Song Publishing,
A division of **Al Menconi Ministries**
Carlsbad, CA 92013
www.AlMenconi.com

First printing 2003
Second printing 2005
© Copyright 2005/2006 **Al Menconi Ministries**
ISBN 0-942925-09-02

Acknowledgements

I would like to thank my wife, Jan, and daughters, Ann and Allison, who continue to teach me how to become the husband and father God has called me to be.

I would like to thank Adina Jaitly, my assistant and trusted "right hand" who challenged every concept and has helped me put this book together.

I would like to thank Norm Daniels for his excellent and insightful drawings.

Most of all, I would like to thank Jesus Christ for giving me a purpose in life.

Introduction

- Did you ever wonder how someone can be "on fire" for Jesus one moment and a few months later that same person isn't even sure if there is a God?

- Have you ever had a "mountain top experience," but can't figure out why you spend most of your life in the "valley?"

- Have you tried living for Jesus, but you just can't seem to do anything right?

- Do you ever feel that everyone is having a "good time" but you?

I can't guarantee that this book will answer all of these questions. That isn't my goal - my goal for this book is to encourage you to think for yourself. I will not tell you what to think, rather, give you questions to equip you to learn how to think for yourself.

Ultimately, life is a series of choices. What are you going to choose?

My hope and prayer is that you will read this book with an open mind and an open heart.

—Al Menconi

"But It Doesn't Affect Me!"

An Honest Look at the Influence of Entertainment

Al Menconi

Chapter 1

One time while on a flight back east, I began talking to a young man who was sitting next to me on the plane. It turned out that we had both attended a Marilyn Manson concert, and we had an interesting conversation about it.

He thought the concert was great. I had a different opinion.
But I didn't want to turn him off, so I just listened and didn't
offer my opinion.

A few minutes into the conversation, I told him that I attended the concert as a concerned Christian. His defenses went up. *"It doesn't affect me!"* He protested. You could almost see him throw his hands up in self-defense!

He acted as if I was getting ready to attack him and he had to defend himself. Obviously, other Christians he had met had tried to cram their opinion of his music down his throat.

Since I was a Christian, he expected me to condemn him too. But I didn't. I simply asked:

"What doesn't affect you?"

He replied, quite sure of himself.

"Really?

How

do

you

know?"

I didn't realize the effect this simple question would have on him. You could almost see the rust coming out of his ears as his brain started to grind, searching frantically to answer my innocent little question.

"Well, I'm not a Satanist!" he said finally. He seemed satisfied that he had given me the final answer to this non-debate debate.

His reasoning seemed logical. *"Marilyn Manson is a Satanist. I listen to Marilyn Manson, but I haven't become a Satanist. Therefore, his music must not affect me."*

"Marilyn Manson isn't a Satanist either!" I replied. You could see the look of surprise on his face.

"He's plays with occult images and he's a sexual pervert, but he's not a Satanist."

"Then he's okay to listen to, right ?"

He quickly sidestepped from being defensive to looking for an excuse.

"It depends,

*...Would you
rather be locked
up in a little room
with a Satanist or
a sexual pervert?"*

When he laughed at my response, I could see he was just looking for a reasonable answer. As we talked, he let his defenses down, and we were able to have normal conversation.

How

about

you?

How

would

you

respond

to

a

reasonable

question

about

your

Entertainment?

Does

your

Entertainment

affect

you?

Really?

How do you know?

Could the **Bible** have a **reasonable** answer to your **entertainment?**

What would you do if God sat down next to you and told you that your entertainment hurt Him?

Would
You
Care?

How about if

God

asked

you

to

change

your

Entertainment?

Would you?

I'm not saying your entertainment has any effect on your life one way or another, but would you be interested in seeing what the Bible says?

Chapter 2

Since you made it this far, I assume you want to see what Scripture says about your entertainment. So let's get right to it.

Colossians 2:8, in a living paraphrase, says:

"Don't let others spoil your faith and joy with their philosophies, their wrong and shallow answers *based on men's thoughts and ideas, instead of on what Christ has said."*

Think about it! Isn't the vast majority of today's entertainment based on some man's, or woman's, thoughts and ideas?

Isn't rock music, or any other style of music, simply some man's or woman's thoughts and ideas written out as lyrics and set to a tune?

THE MOVIES

Aren't motion pictures, television programs, and videos simply some man's or woman's thoughts and ideas put on celluloid and then shown on a screen?

Have you ever thought about this? Before *Grand Theft Auto* and other video games became so popular, they were somebody's thoughts and ideas.

Isn't

That

True?

So what?

The **Bible** says you will spoil your **faith** and **joy** if you keep shoving the **empty philosophies** of this world into your **mind.**

That's what.

With so much of today's entertainment based on thoughts and ideas that are against what the Bible has to say, it seems reasonable to ask the following questions:

- **How is your faith in Jesus Christ?**

- **Do you ever think that you've lost your salvation?**

- **Do you wonder if there is a God?**

- **Is Jesus God?**

- **Is the Bible true?**

- **Do you ever have problems with your faith?**

No?

That's

Great!

How's your *joy?*

Do you have...

love,
joy,
peace,
gentleness,
kindness,
hope,
patience,
etc.,
etc.
that's part of *the Fruit of the Spirit.*

Galatians 5:22+23

"But the fruit of the Spirit is...

love,

joy,

peace,

patience,

kindness,
goodness,
faithfulness,
gentleness,
and
self-control..."

All together they are called *joy*.

Does *joy* radiate in your life?

No?

Why
not?

Maybe you have been allowing

someone

else

to

undermine

your

Faith

in

Jesus

and

the

Joy

of

your

salvation

through

their philosophies.

48

Chapter 3

Did you realize that when you committed your life to Christ and joined the Kingdom of Light,

Satan declared war on you?

It is a spiritual war for your *mind.*

Most Christians don't realize they are in a war for control of their mind. If they knew what Satan was doing, they would set up some defenses and be ready for him.

14. THE ALAMO, BUILT 1718, SAN ANTONIO, TEXAS

BUT he isn't going to warn you that you are in a war.

He's just going to start shooting.

And he aims his ammunition **(his philosophies)** from the most unsuspecting places.

He uses much of today's entertainment media as weapons aimed directly at our **faith** and **joy**.

The world of entertainment isn't the only battlefield, but it's one of the most important ones — especially to young people! Is Satan winning this battle in your life?

Remember!

<u>Satan hates you!</u>

He would destroy you completely if he could.
But he can't. God won't let him.
So he uses sneaky tricks on us.
Since he can't destroy our Christianity,
He'll settle for weakening it instead.

Chapter 4

When I first became a Christian, I expected to be covered in so much of God's goodness and rightness that I would be perfect.

I wasn't.

I tried to be *"good"* but I couldn't stop thinking and doing things that I knew wouldn't make God happy.

When I realized I wasn't perfect, I started to wonder if God had come into my life at all!

At first I didn't realize that this was

one
of
Satan's
best
tricks
to
fool
Christians.

Then I read what the Bible had to say:

Romans 8:38+39

"For I am convinced that neither death nor life, neither angels nor demons, neither the present nor the future, nor any powers, neither height nor depth, nor anything else in all creation, will be able to separate us from the love of God that is in Christ Jesus our Lord."

In other words,

GOD
WILL
NEVER
LEAVE
US!

- EVER

I found out that when we commit our life to Jesus, He will never forsake us or leave us. **NOTHING** can separate us from the love of God.

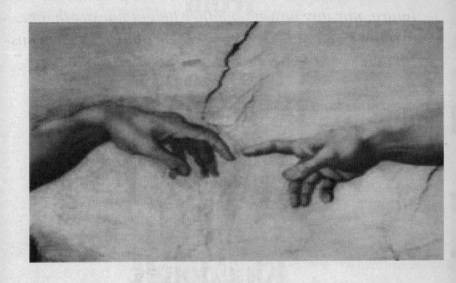

NOTHING!

We have been transferred from the kingdom of darkness to the Kingdom of Light.

Read

Colossians 1:13

"For He delivered us from the power of darkness, and transferred us into the Kingdom of His Son!"

You can look it up for yourself.

Colossians is close to the middle of the New Testament, just

after Philippians and just before I Thessalonians

1. Satan has lost us forever!

2. He can't get us back.

3. So the next best thing he can do

is

to

make

us

ineffective

and

weak.

What makes a Christian **strong?**

Nehemiah 8:10 says...

"...the Joy of the Lord is our strength".

It's not just the title of a song you sang in Sunday school or at summer camp.

The Joy of the Lord **IS** what makes you spiritually strong.

Our **strength** comes when we
have the Joy of the Lord ...

*The
Fruit
of
the
Spirit*

...in our lives.

If the opposite of strength is the **lack of strength** – or weakness – then the opposite of Joy is the **lack of Joy.**

If **Satan is going to make us weak and ineffective,** he's going to have to spoil our **Faith and Joy**.

That's why Scripture warns us in Colossians 2:8:

"...don't let others spoil your **faith** *and* **joy** *with their philosophies, their wrong and shallow answers based on men's thoughts and ideas, instead of on what Christ has said."*

Why?

Because if we let this happen to us, we will become weak and ineffective!

Weak Christian

A quick review:

How does Satan weaken a Christian?

By getting us to entertain ourselves with the empty philosophies of this world, based on men's thoughts and ideas, instead of what the Bible teaches.

Where

do

you

find

these

philosophies?

Television programs

Movies

Videos

Music and

Video games

are excellent breeding grounds.

Think about it. If you were Satan, what would YOU do to weaken a Christian's faith and joy?

?

?   ?

?

?

?

First, you would pretend to be the Christian's friend.

Then you would try to poison **(weaken)** the Christian so

he wouldn't be dangerous **(strong)** to you.

You would be clever enough to hide your poison by mixing it

in something the Christian consumes everyday.

That's exactly what Satan has done to us! He has put his empty **(poison)** philosophies in much of our entertainment so we can literally

entertain ourselves to death.

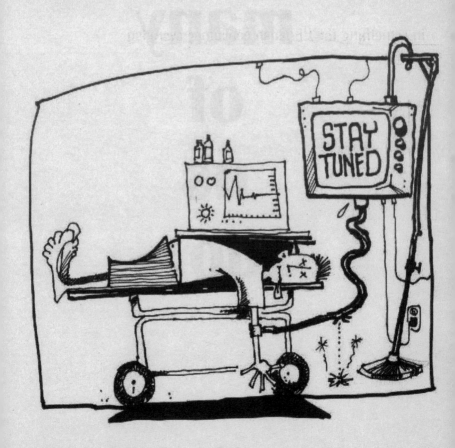

And many of us do.

On a scale of 1 to 10, how is your **faith in Jesus** and the **joy of your salvation?**

Just enough to get by?

Less than a ten?

Did you ever think that maybe God meant for you to be a level **10** Christian? Are you living for Him at a level **1** because you entertained the other nine levels to death?

The level 1 Christian hasn't lost his salvation, but is Satan winning the battle for his mind?

Do you think this guy is struggling with his faith and joy?

Chapter 5

I'm not saying your salvation comes from works.

We
    are
        saved
            by

God's Grace

and not of any works we have done!

> *"For it is by grace you have been saved, through faith—and this not from yourselves, it is the gift of God – not by works, so that no one can boast."* — **Ephesians 2:8+9**

But we have a responsibility to **GrOW**

spiritually!
    If
    we
    don't
    grow,
    we
    will
    remain
    spiritual
    babies
    our
    whole
    life.

Some people think that if they grow spiritually in Christ, they will be uncool and miss out on all the "fun" the world's system offers.

If that's what you're thinking, consider this.

When we see a baby in a crib that's just a few weeks old, he just lies there and coos, *"Goo-goo"* and *"Ga-ga."* This makes us smile and say, *"Isn't he cute?!"*

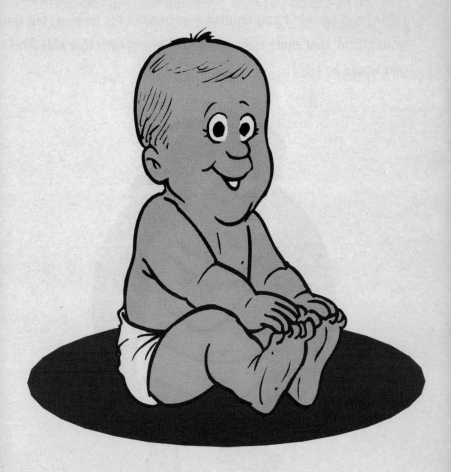

But what if you went back ten years later, and this same baby is now ten years old and is still in his crib saying, *"Goo-goo"* and *"Ga-ga?"* Would you say this was still cute? If you were polite, you wouldn't say anything in front of his mother, but you would think that there was something wrong with this kid! And you would be right.

You see, we have a reasonable expectation of seeing a child grow and when we don't see any growth, the assumption is that something is terribly wrong.

Are you growing in Christ?

How would people respond to you?

Are

you

acting

your

spiritual

age?

Chapter 6

Try to imagine a clean sheet of paper.

The kind of paper doesn't matter as long as it is clean and usable. Kind of like the next page

It could be an 8 1/2" x 11" sheet of copy paper or maybe it's the little note size paper that mothers...

_____

_____

_____

_____

_____

_____

_____

_____

_____

_____

_____

_____

_____

_____

_____

_____

_____

_____

_____

...use to write thank you notes.

What would happen to that clean sheet if you lit a match,

blew out the flame

and set the hot ash immediately on the paper?

P.S. Please don't try this at home!

It wouldn't burn the paper completely, but it would scorch it a little and leave a little scar.

You wouldn't like it, but you would hardly notice one little scar.

You still might be able to write a letter on it and send it to someone without anyone noticing.

What would happen if someone lit another match and set it down on your writing paper, and another and another and another, until the paper was covered with burn marks?

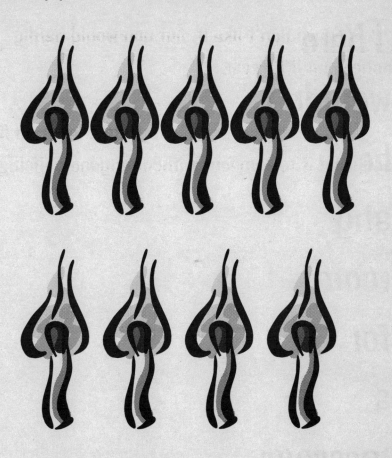

Could you use it for a letter?

No way!

There
wouldn't
be
any
room
for
a
message.

Your mind is like that sheet of paper. Each scar represents sinful, wrong thoughts and attitudes that have been burned into your mind.

When you accept Christ as your Savior, He comes in and begins healing the scars with the ointment of His **Grace**.

As you allow Him to control more and more of your life, He is able to heal more and more of the scars.

This is called

spiritual

Growth

But what if, as Christ applied the ointment of His Word to your scars, you continued to add more and more burnt matches by filling your brain (writing paper) with the empty philosophies of this world? That's right. Very little progress would be made.

He will continue to be in your life, but in order for progress to be made, you have to stop burning your "paper"—

you have to stop scarring your mind.

When you accept Jesus as your Lord and Savior, the process of healing your brain

(the renewing of your mind – **Romans 12:1-2**) begins.

*"...don't be conformed to the values of this world, but **be transformed by the renewing of your mind!**"*

At the same time, Satan wants to weaken you and make you less effective for the Kingdom of God. Satan tempts you to keep adding matches, but because you now belong to Christ you have the choice to

Just say no.

"You show that you are a letter from Christ, the result of our ministry, written not with ink but with the Spirit of the living God, not on tablets of stone but on tablets of human hearts." **II Corinthians 3:3**

We are God's writing tablets.

He wants to use us to send "love letters" from Him to the world. People are "reading" our lives. Is that cool or what?

What do they read when they read you?

What is on your writing tablet?

Is it clean and filled with His message? Or is it scarred beyond recognition?

The
Choice
is
yours.

Remember, life is a series of choices.

What are you choosing?

Chapter 7

Now maybe you're thinking that it's just a movie or just a television program or just a song or just a video game.

How can that possibly affect my faith in Jesus and the joy of my salvation?

"I'm not joining in it. I'm simply using it to entertain myself for a while."

Please allow me to respond with a story of two little boys.

Billy and Bobby were on a playground at recess. Billy started telling a dirty joke. Bobby, who was a Christian, wanted to walk away, but the joke was funny, so he stayed. He tried not to laugh, but it was really funny. *"That wasn't so bad,"* he thought. *"And besides, I'm not the one telling the jokes, I'm just listening."*

Then Billy told another dirty joke and Bobby laughed again. When Billy saw that Bobby was laughing at the dirty jokes, he started adding profanity to make it more interesting. And Bobby continued to laugh. Billy told another and another until the bell rang ending recess.

When they got to their classroom, Bobby raised his hand for the teacher to call on him.

"Miss Jones, Billy was telling dirty jokes at recess." Bobby proclaimed.

What do you suppose Billy said in his defense?

"Yeah, but Bobby was laughing!"

In other words,

"Bobby's as guilty as I am because his laughter showed he was actively participating in what I was saying."

That's exactly what Satan is trying to get us to do.

If he can get us to laugh, cry, get excited, tap our foot, or generally enjoy his tune or story, we are mentally participating in the activity– just like Bobby.

Maybe you believe that when you play, watch, or listen to sex scenes, violence, or profanity, they don't bother you.

Why don't they bother you?

They bother God!

Ephesians 4:29

Chapter 8

Much of today's **entertainment** media literally **encourages** us to become a nation of **Perverts!**

Before you jump ship from my logic, think about

The following illustration.

What would you think of someone who spends his evenings prowling around neighborhoods, peering into windows, watching couples have sex?

Would you consider this guy a pervert?

I would!

Isn't that what much of today's entertainment does to our mind's eye?

It takes our mind into other people's bedrooms to watch them have sex. Or into their bathrooms to watch them urinate, play with themselves, or get their private parts caught in a zipper!

This behavior is acceptable in the world of entertainment because it is "funny."

Is
it
really
acceptable
behavior
for
you?

I thought we decided that **people** who looked in on others private matters were **acting like perverts.**

Are you saying:

Perversion
is
acceptable?

Chapter 9

"Okay, maybe a lot of today's entertainment is perverted and immoral, but I don't let it affect me!"

Add that excuse to *"I just like the beat,"* and you have the most frequently used excuse used by today's young adult. *"It doesn't affect me, you didn't see it affect me, and you can't prove it affects me."* No one ever wants to admit that their entertainment affects them in a negative way...

I have

3

responses:

Response #1.

*How
do
you
know
it
doesn't
affect
you?*

God's
Word
doesn't
say
you'll
be
a
pervert
if
you
watch

Perversion

He doesn't say you'll be

Depressed and **Angry**

if you listen to

Depressing and **Angry**

music.

God doesn't say you will

kill people

if you play

"First person shooter"

games.

And He doesn't say

you'll become a

homosexual

if you entertain yourself

with

homosexuals.

God's Word says...

if you choose to entertain yourself with the

Empty
Philosophies

of this world,

you will struggle

with your

faith and joy.

How is your

faith

in

Jesus?

(Do you ever think that you have lost your salvation?
Do you ever wonder if there is a God? Is Jesus Christ God?)

How is the
Joy
of
your
salvation?

(Love, joy, peace, patience, kindness, goodness, faithfulness, gentleness, self-control)

and...

What are you entertaining yourself with?

(Television, movies, video, music, Internet, computer games)

Response #2.

Much of today's music and other forms of entertainment are just like a

Commercial.

Think about it!

What's the difference between a

Music Video

and a

Mountain Dew,

Gap Jeans or

Volkswagen

commercial?

If you said about

three minutes,

you would be right.

30 seconds = **commercial**

3 ½ minutes = **music video**

In about 30 seconds, advertisers for

Mountain Dew,
Gap Jeans, or
Volkswagen, etc.

sell us their soft drinks, clothes and cars by using:

- Music with a good beat,
- cute girls, and
- fast video clips.

In 3 ½ minutes, music videos use the same methods:

- Music with a good beat,
- cute girls, and
- fast video clips.

If **Mountain Dew**, and other advertisers are able to sell you their product in 30 seconds, don't you think a video could sell you its product in 3 ½ minutes?

Yes, they can and they do!

What
is
their
"product?"

It's the

philosophy

of the

writer

and/or the

performer.

"But I'm not buying it?"

Really?

Reread response #1

(on page 131)

147

Response #3.

Much of today's entertainment is a very effective audio/visual education tool.

Audio/visual equipment like:

Televisions, DVD players, iPods,

And especially

Video games

are some of the most effective teaching tools used in the classroom.

When teachers use these tools in a classroom, they can see learning taking place by their students.

But what would you call these tools if we took them out of the classroom and put them into your home?

They would still be
**Televisions,
DVDs/Videos,
CD Players, iPods**
And **Video Games.**

If they are effective teaching tools in the **classroom,** they are effective teaching tools in your **home.**

What's that?

You don't think they are teaching you anything?

No?

Reread response #1.

(on page 131)

Chapter 10

I am not saying the entertainment media is the only way for turning empty and perverted philosophies into your mind. It just seems to be the most effective way. I'm not saying it is a sin to watch television, listen to rock music, or entertain yourself with today's entertainment.

But...

When you do, be aware of the poison of empty philosophies that are being fed to you as a form of entertainment.

Psalm 19:14

*"May the words of my mouth
and the*

meditation of my heart

*be pleasing in your sight,
O Lord,
my Rock
and my Redeemer."*

What are you meditating on?

Is it pleasing to God?

Psalm 19:14

encourages

us

to

let

our

thoughts

be

pleasing

to

God,

so

we

will

know

His

peace.

Is
your
heart
at
Peace?

Chapter 11

How can we obtain more **PEACE**
in our lives?

1) By making choices that God wants for us.

2) By making decisions consistent with God's Word.

How can we make wiser decisions
about our entertainment?

Let me introduce you to

The Teeter-Totter Principle

A teeter-totter (or see-saw) is a straight board balanced on a fulcrum.

When weight is placed on either side of the board, it will naturally tilt to the side with the most weight.

On a spiritual teeter-totter, the board is our spiritual life. The fulcrum is **Colossians 2:8** which says,

> "Don't let others spoil your **faith** and **joy** with their philosophies, wrong and shallow answers based on men's thoughts and ideas, instead of on what Christ has said."

Colossians 2:8

This is the balancing point by which we can measure the weight / impact of entertainment in our Christian lives.

On one side of the teeter-totter are the empty philosophies of the world.

No philosophy is emptier than the

Satanic Bible.

On the other side are the philosophies that bring

life and peace.

These obviously come from the

Holy Bible.

The number **#1** teaching from the

Satanic Bible is

"Live for yourself.
Fulfill your lustful desires.
If it feels good, do it."

The next highest law from the **Satanic Bible**
says to deny biblical values (deny Jesus as Lord).

Simply stated in five words,

"Live For Self – Deny Jesus."

On the right side of the board is the philosophy of Jesus:

"If anyone would come after me, he must deny himself, take up his cross, and follow me."

Matthew 16:24.

Simply stated in five words,

"Deny Self, Live For Jesus."

Can you see how the philosophies of the **Holy Bible** and the **Satanic Bible** are total opposites?

Live
For
Self,
Deny
Jesus

vs.

Live
For
Jesus,
Deny
Self

Where does your entertainment fit on the

Teeter-totter

of your life?

What are the philosophies of your favorite...

Music,

Television shows,

Movies,

DVDs/Videos, and/or

Video games?

Are they closer to the

Satanic Bible   or the   Holy Bible?

Does the **philosophy** and/or lifestyle of your favorite performer or movie or program or game

feed your selfish desires

or does it

feed your soul?

Does your entertainment
Teeter?

or Totter?

You know how a teeter-totter works. If you put more weight on one side than the other, the heaviest side will sink to the ground.

Some Christians think they are in balance if they entertain themselves with an equal amount of godly philosophies and ungodly philosophies on their entertainment teeter-totter.

The Bible says that isn't **balance**,

that is spiritual **wishy-washy.**

Revelation 3:16 says:

"Because you are lukewarm, neither hot nor cold, I am about to spit you out of my mouth."

If your entertainment teeter-totter is leaning toward the teeter side, there is a good chance your spiritual life is leaning that way as well.

That's
why
I
suggest
going
on
a
diet.

A
Christian
Music
Diet

To help you live *FullTilt* for Jesus!

Chapter 12

Do you remember when you were a little kid on a teeter totter and the big kid on the other side would have his end on the ground? Your feet would be dangling up in the air!

Only when your big friend got off, were your feet able to touch the ground again.

That's the principle of the Christian Music Diet — to help you to *Live FullTilt* for Jesus.

The Christian Music Diet

- It's designed to help you get back on your spiritual feet and clean up your mind.

- For the next thirty days, I challenge you to eliminate all music and other forms of entertainment that are **against** biblical values, and only listen to godly music.

- That's it.

I'm not saying that everything else is evil. I'm simply saying that doing this will help you see life from a more godly perspective. It's just common sense.

Q: Can't I simply try to listen to better music and not watch bad movies?

A: You can, but you will probably continue to struggle with your faith and your joy. We need a simple plan and it doesn't get any simpler than **The Christian Music Diet.**

Without a plan you can say, "I've got to eat less fattening food" without knowing what food was fattening. What I am suggesting is to eliminate all your "old food" (because much of it i "fattening") and only eat "new and approved" food for thirty days. It eliminates all decisions and questions. When in doubt, leave it out.

It is our hope that after 30 days, you will be able to recognize which of the foods you have been "eating" are "fattening."

I'm afraid that since our mind has been immersed in the mind pollution of the world of entertainment, we probably have a difficult time telling tell the difference between what is good and what isn't.

"But
If
I
Do
What
You
Are
Suggesting,
Isn't
That
A
Form
Of
Brain-washing?"

Yes!

When you wash your brain with
Truth
it will help you have a clean brain!!

Brain wash,

wash brain,

CLEAN BRAIN

At the end of **30 days** of listening

exclusively to **godly music**, see if you

aren't better focused to **make wiser**

Entertainment

choices that won't be

poisoning your **Faith in Christ**

and the **Joy** of your salvation.

When all is said and done,

remember the problem is **NOT**

Marilyn Manson,

Grand Theft Auto,

and other ungodly entertainment,

and

the

answer

is

NOT

listening

Christian

music.

The problem is

Sin

And the answer is

Jesus

Your

Entertainment

can

either

help

you

focus on life from man's point of view

or

it

can

help

you

focus

on

the

Author of Life

The

Choice

Is

yours.

Are you ready to live

FullTilt

for Jesus?

If you liked this book, why not share it with someone you care about...

...not someone you think is wrong